I0055425

Praise for Dean Crisp

"This the book is amazing and is the simple key to opening the leadership world. If you used these truths and you have the self motivation you will succeed at anything."

— Artie Newhook, Deputy Chief of
Berkley PD in Massachusetts

"Dean is passionate, knowledgeable, and full of experience and wisdom."

— John Paul Cartier (from Phoenix, AZ)

"Dean built a fire in me to strive to be significant every day in everything I do. Dean pushes you way out of your comfort zone and into greatness."

— Christy Shaffer (from Phoenix, AZ)

"Dean is a fantastic speaker and his knowledge and wisdom is immediately recognizable. He is engaging and the information is captivating. It was so refreshing to listen to someone that is real, genuine, and has 'been there, done that.'"

— Zack Lewis (from Phoenix, AZ)

"Dean Crisp has a lifetime of knowledge to pass on that I feel would lead to effective leadership in any organization."

— John Darling (from Phoenix, AZ)

"Dean has a way of relating leadership qualities to both your life at home and in the workplace."

— Jeremy Knoll (from Tucson, AZ)

"Dean knows how to bring out the best in you and make you truly evaluate who you are."

— Peter Cazeau (from Boston, MA)

5 Simple Truths of Leadership

Also by Dean Crisp

Essential Leadership Lessons from the Thin Blue Line

The Leadership Recipe

5 Simple Truths of Leadership

HOW TO BE A SIGNIFICANT LEADER IN YOUR BUSINESS, ORGANIZATION, AND LIFE

Dean Crisp

Torchflame Books

Vista, CA

Copyright © 2025 by Dean Crisp

All rights reserved. Torchflame Books supports copyright. Copyright fuels creativity, encourages diverse voices, promotes free speech, and creates a vibrant culture. Thank you for buying an authorized edition of this book and for complying with copyright laws by not reproducing, scanning, or distributing any part of it in any form without permission, except by a reviewer who wishes to quote brief passages in connection with a review written for insertion in a magazine, newspaper, broadcast, website, blog or other outlet. You are supporting independent publishing and allowing Torchflame Books to publish books for all readers.

NO AI TRAINING: Without in any way limiting the author's [and publisher's] exclusive rights under copyright, any use of this publication to "train" generative artificial intelligence (AI) technologies to generate text is expressly prohibited. The author reserves all rights to license uses of this work for generative AI training and development of machine learning language models.

ISBN: 978-1-61153-691-1 (hardcover)

ISBN: 978-1-61153-690-4 (ebook)

ISBN: 978-1-61153-689-8 (large print)

Library of Congress Control Number: 2025903828

5 *Simple Truths of Leadership* is published by: Torchflame Books, an imprint of Top Reads Publishing, LLC, 1035 E. Vista Way, Suite 205, Vista, CA 92084, USA

Cover design and interior layout: Jori Hanna

Cover image and interior illustrations: Adobe Stock

The publisher is not responsible for websites or social media accounts (or their content) that are not owned by the publisher.

Contents

"

The Five Simple Truths are not just concepts—they are a roadmap. They are the reason I have been able to navigate the ups and downs of my career and achieve success on my terms. And now, I'm sharing them with you, because I believe they can do the same for you.

A Moment of Reflection: Where It All Began

Several years ago, I was traveling through Wyoming to teach a leadership class. It was my first visit to this part of the country, and I was struck by the vast, open landscape. There was a raw beauty to Wyoming that seemed to stretch endlessly—a fitting backdrop for reflection. But I wasn't thinking about reflection that evening. I was thinking about getting to my final destination, and my journey to get there had been grueling.

The day had started with a long flight from Asheville, North Carolina, to Denver, Colorado. What should have been a routine trip was derailed by delays that left me landing late on a Sunday night. To make matters more challenging, my final destination was a three-hour drive from the airport. By the time I reached my hotel, it was nearly 3 a.m.

I normally like to start my mornings with a run or some form of exercise, especially when traveling. But after such a long day, I skipped my morning routine and dove straight into teaching. It wasn't until that afternoon after wrapping up a full day of class that I laced up my running shoes and headed out for a run.

The small town where I was staying was surrounded by Wyoming's unique terrain—a mix of flat plains and rolling hills. I wound up running through quiet neighborhoods, letting the rhythm of my steps match the stillness of the place. As I ran, I passed a car parked along the road, and it stopped me in my tracks.

The car looked exactly like the one I drove as a young detective—a 1979 Chevrolet Nova, four-door. Except for the color, it was identical to the vehicle that had been my companion during the early years of my career. Seeing that car was like stepping into a time machine. Suddenly, I was no longer in Wyoming but back on the streets of my hometown as a young cop navigating the challenges of those early days.

Standing there, staring at that car, I felt the weight of the past years in a single moment. It was as if time had collapsed, bringing the past and present face to face. "How did I get from there to here?' I asked myself. "How did I go from being a young detective driving that car to where I was now—teaching leadership, serving as a police chief, speaking nationally, and running two businesses?"

That question stayed with me as I finished my run and returned to the hotel. The moment was too powerful to ignore. I grabbed a notepad and began writing down everything I could think of—what had helped me grow, what had shaped me, and what had guided me along the way.

What I discovered that night was life-changing. As I wrote, the patterns became clear. It wasn't luck or chance that had propelled me forward. It wasn't simply being in the right place at the right time. My success had been built on a foundation of principles—simple truths that I had followed, often without even realizing it. What I also discovered was that anyone can use them to propel themselves to be successful and significant, which is why I am sharing them with you today.

The Birth of the Five Simple Truths

That late-night reflection in Wyoming was the moment this book was born. As I sat there, scribbling down my thoughts, I realized that the path I had taken was not random. It was a deliberate journey shaped by choices, actions, and values.

I kept coming back to five key principles—truths that had guided me through every challenge, every opportunity, and every success. These weren't complicated ideas; they were straightforward, practical, and timeless. They were the foundation of my leadership journey, and they became the framework for this book:

1. **Direction** – Knowing where you're headed. Without it, you're simply drifting.

2. **Intentionality** – Acting with purpose and making deliberate choices that align with your goals.

3. **Teams** – Building strong relationships and

surrounding yourself with people who believe in the mission.

4. **Standards** – Holding yourself and others to a high level of excellence.

5. **Getting Ahead of Your Day** – Preparing, planning, and starting each day with clarity and purpose.

As I wrote about these truths, I realized they were not just principles for leadership—they were principles for life. They helped me grow as a leader, achieve my goals, and make an impact in ways I never imagined.

Why This Story Matters

I share this story because it is a reminder that leadership is a journey, not a destination. It's about taking the time to reflect on where you have been, where you are, and where you're going. That moment in Wyoming was a turning point for me. It forced me to pause and think about what had worked in my life and why.

The Five Simple Truths are not just concepts—they are a roadmap. They are the reason I have been able to navigate the ups and downs of my career and achieve success on my terms. And now, I'm sharing them with you, because I believe they can do the same for you.

No matter where you are in your leadership journey, these truths will give you the clarity, focus, and tools you need to lead with purpose, build strong teams, and create a lasting impact.

Introduction

The Five Simple Truths of Leadership

Leadership is one of the most profound callings a person can undertake. It is the art of guiding, influencing, and inspiring others toward a shared purpose, often in the face of challenges and uncertainty. Great leadership is not about a title or position; it is about character, intentional action, and the ability to create a lasting impact on others.

At its core, leadership is about becoming significant —a leader who doesn't just lead, but leaves a legacy. A significant leader is someone who inspires others to rise above mediocrity, who shapes teams into forces of collective strength, and who consistently embodies values that others want to emulate. But what does it take to become such a leader?

The path to significant leadership is not as complicated as you might think. In my decades of experience leading organizations, mentoring others, and navigating the complexities of leadership, I have found that the principles behind great leadership are often simple. These are not abstract theories or fleeting trends. They are enduring truths that apply to leaders in every industry, role, and stage of life. This book is about those truths.

Why Leadership Needs Truths

Leadership is full of noise—competing advice, strategies, and opinions on what works best. While the world changes rapidly, the core of what makes a great leader remains constant. It is easy to lose sight of what really matters amid distractions, but "truths" are the anchors that keep us grounded.

A truth, by definition, is something fundamental and enduring. It does not change with circumstances or trends. Truths form the foundation of our decisions, actions, and beliefs. They guide us in the right direction, even when the path ahead is uncertain. They are true even if you don't practice them, apply them, or use them. There are many truths in the world we live in and the truths that I discuss in this book are so simple and easy to understand as well as apply to your leadership. Truths will stand when all else fails.

The Five Simple Truths presented in this book are the building blocks of significant leadership. They are not shortcuts or hacks. Instead, they are proven principles that reflect the timeless qualities of great leaders.

By understanding and applying these truths, you create a framework for leading with clarity, consistency, and purpose.

Why These Truths Matter

The Five Simple Truths are not just tools; they are pathways to greatness. Each truth builds upon the others, creating a powerful synergy. For example, you can have a clear direction, but without intentionality, your vision remains just a dream. You can build a strong team, but without high standards, the team may falter.

These truths work together to address every aspect of leadership:

- Direction - creates clarity
- Intentionality - creates momentum
- Teams - creates strength
- Standards - creates excellence
- Getting Ahead of Your Day - creates control

When you embrace these truths, you align your leadership with timeless principles that ensure sustained impact and success. You guarantee your significance.

The Five Simple Truths

The framework of this book is built around five essential truths that form the foundation of significant leadership:

1. **Direction** – Leadership begins with clarity of purpose. A leader must know where they are going before they can guide others. Direction is about having a vision, setting goals, and ensuring that every action aligns with those objectives. Without direction, you are merely reacting to circumstances rather than creating a future.

2. **Intentionality** – Leadership is not accidental. It requires deliberate choices and consistent effort. Intentionality is about focusing your energy on what matters most, making purposeful decisions, and showing up every day with the determination to move closer to your goals.

3. Teams – No leader succeeds alone. Building and nurturing a strong team is at the heart of significant leadership. Whether it's a small group or an entire organization, the power of collaboration, trust, and shared purpose is what drives success.

4. Standards – Great leaders hold themselves and their teams to high standards. They don't settle for "good enough." They push for excellence, inspire others to strive for greatness, and create an environment where high standards are the norm.

5. Getting Ahead of Your Day – Leadership thrives on preparation. Significant leaders don't wait for the day to dictate their actions; they set the tone from the start.

By planning, prioritizing, and taking control of your time, you can lead with focus and resilience.

These Five Simple Truths are more than just principles; they are a playbook for leadership. Whether you're leading a small team, an entire organization, or simply leading yourself, these truths will help you and others become more intentional, impactful, and significant.

The Structure of the Book

This book is structured to help you understand not only what leadership is, but how to become significant in your leadership journey by applying the Five Simple Truths. After defining what leadership really means in the opening chapter, we will explore each truth in detail. Along the way, I will share practical tips, real-world examples, and stories of leaders who have applied these truths to achieve incredible results.

How The Book is Organized

Introduction: Leadership Defined – This chapter sets the stage by exploring the meaning of leadership and why it is important to define your own version of significance before embarking on any journey.

Chapters 1–6: The Five Simple Truths – Each of these chapters will focus on one of the Five Simple Truths. We will begin with Direction, because without a clear direction, none of the other truths can function. From there, we will dive into Intentionality, Teams, Standards, and Getting Ahead of Your Day. Each truth will be explored with real-world applications, tips, and exercises you can use to implement these principles in your own life.

Being a Significant Leader – A Call to Lasting Impact

In both personal and professional life, the drive to make a lasting impact sets exceptional leaders apart. We don't just want to achieve success for ourselves; we want our work to be meaningful and enduring. A significant leader strives for purpose beyond accolades, fostering positive change, lifting others, and leaving a legacy that continues well beyond their tenure. Leaders who embrace this mindset shift from pursuing individual success to embodying genuine purpose, integrity, and deep influence.

The goal of this book is to guide you on the journey to becoming a significant leader. Using the Five Simple Truths as a foundation—Direction, Intentionality, Teams, Standards, and Getting Ahead of Your Day—you will gain a roadmap for creating lasting impact. These principles are practical and accessible to anyone willing to dedicate themselves to the pursuit of purposeful leadership. Each truth, when practiced consistently, helps transform leadership from a position of authority to a powerful, service-oriented journey.

Defining Significance in Leadership

Success often appears as a checklist of accomplishments or promotions, but leadership significance is far more profound. It means discovering purpose, aligning with values, and positively impacting others through each decision, task, and challenge. A significant leader doesn't just accumulate achievements—they set an example, live out their values, and build others up along the way.

Consider the example of General Colin Powell, a leader who understood that significance wasn't about rank but about respect, integrity, and creating a standard others could aspire to. Powell's commitment to purposeful leadership and ethical values shows the essence of being a significant leader. His example of humility, decisiveness, and honesty continues to inspire leaders who want their impact to transcend individual success.

True leadership significance emerges from intentional choices, daily actions, and a mindset that values purpose over titles. With this understanding, the Five Simple Truths become the pillars that help us build lives and careers of real influence.

The Five Simple Truths as the Path to Becoming a Significant Leader

Significant leadership is not about fleeting victories or isolated achievements; it's about sustained influence and a legacy of quality. It's about doing what other leaders can't do. It's about being in the top ten percent of leaders in your organization or selected field. The Five Simple Truths provide a blueprint for this purpose. When practiced, they transform leadership from a set of tasks into a fulfilling journey of enduring impact.

Direction – A significant leader knows where they are going and why. Without direction, purpose is lost. Direction is not just about goals but about aligning those goals with values and a vision that resonates with others.

Intentionality – With direction in place, intentionality fuels the journey. Significant leaders act with purpose, making deliberate choices and seeking opportunities to grow themselves and those around them. They don't wait for success to happen; they create it.

Teams – Effective leaders know they cannot achieve significance alone. They build teams united by a shared vision, investing in each person's growth. A significant leader knows that true power comes from empowering others.

Standards – The standards we uphold define our level of significance. By setting high expectations, we challenge ourselves and our teams to strive for excellence. Significant leaders attract and inspire high achievers, fostering a culture of integrity and improvement.

Getting Ahead of Your Day – Preparation and clarity allow significant leaders to manage each day's challenges with intention. By planning ahead, they ensure they can be proactive, resilient, and fully engaged with their team. Leading from a place of preparation builds confidence in others and allows a leader to navigate unexpected changes with grace.

Moving from Success to Significant Leadership

Being successful as a leader is a noble and appropriate goal to achieve. I define being a successful leader as one who makes sure those they are leading are successful. Being successful is important, but it is not enough. As a significant leader, you are ensuring that the next generation of leaders are mentored and led to be the best of the best. Understanding the Five Simple Truths and applying them are key characteristics in making sure that others are a success. But being successful is simply not enough. You must be significant in your leadership. Leaders like Angela Merkel and Malala Yousafzai illustrate the difference between individual success and significant leadership. Merkel, as Germany's Chancellor, focused on unity, purpose, and values—her impact extends beyond any single achievement. Malala's advocacy for girls' education wasn't for personal gain but a commitment to a cause far greater than herself. In both cases, these leaders demonstrate that significance comes from unwavering values and commitment to a purpose that benefits others.

Building Significance through the Five Simple Truths

By embodying the Five Simple Truths, leaders develop purpose-driven lives and careers. These truths are dynamic and adaptable, offering tools to help every leader navigate their unique journey. Each chapter in this book builds upon these principles, creating a complete framework for significant leadership.

Why This Book Matters

This book is both a guide and a companion to your leadership journey. It's not only about learning skills, but about cultivating a mindset focused on purpose, consistency, and service. The Five Simple Truths form a pathway toward significant leadership, shaping you into a leader who not only reaches goals but leaves a lasting legacy. Leadership is a skill, but it's also a mindset and a way of life. By embracing the Five Simple Truths, you will not only elevate your own leadership but also inspire those around you to achieve their best. Are you ready to embark on a journey to becoming a successful and significant leader? This book will show you how.

Let's begin.

———— 66 ————

Direction is not about having a perfect plan.
It's about having a purpose and trusting
that the steps you take will lead you closer
to where you're meant to be.

Chapter 1
Direction: The First Simple Truth

DIRECTION IS ONE OF THE MOST FUND-
amental human needs—it is as essential to our well-
being as food or shelter. Deep within us is an innate
desire to move forward, to make progress, and to find
purpose in the journey. Every waking moment of our
lives, whether we realize it or not, we're always
heading somewhere. The moment you wake up, your
day begins to unfold along a certain path. By the time
your head hits the pillow at night, your mind is already
churning about what's next.

But direction is not just about movement; it's about
purpose and meaning. Imagine wandering aimlessly
through a dense forest with no map, no compass, and
no destination in mind. Sure, you're moving, but
without a sense of direction, every step you take feels
uncertain and wasted. The same is true in leadership.
Without direction, even the most vigorous efforts can
lead to stagnation, frustration, or failure. Direction

ensures that every step you take, every decision you make, is purposeful and aligned with a greater vision.

Direction provides more than just a path—it offers clarity. It eliminates the noise of distractions and competing priorities, allowing you to focus on what truly matters. This clarity builds momentum, and with momentum comes progress. Leaders with direction inspire confidence because they know where they are going and can articulate why it matters.

The importance of direction cannot be overstated in leadership. It's the compass that keeps you steady when the storms of life and work threaten to derail you. It's the lighthouse that guides your team when uncertainty looms. Direction is not just about setting goals; it's about understanding your "why" and aligning your actions with your purpose. A leader with clear direction transforms motion into progress and ambition into achievement. Without it, even the most well-intentioned efforts can feel like treading water.

Direction gives meaning to movement, turning ordinary actions into extraordinary accomplishments. It's not just about getting from Point A to Point B—it's about ensuring that every step taken between those points is purposeful, deliberate, and impactful.

As humans, we're natural explorers—wired to seek, discover, and make sense of the world. Direction gives us the focus and drive to do just that. But here is the thing: direction doesn't need to be rigid, like a GPS route that never wavers. Life is organic. It's messy, full of unexpected turns and course corrections. Direction is not about knowing every single step you will take; it's about making sure you're consistently steering toward a positive outcome.

Let's be honest—knowing where you're headed as a leader can feel overwhelming, even impossible. You have dreams, ambitions, and this drive to make an impact, but sometimes you don't even know what the next step looks like. I get it. I have been there.

When I first felt the desire to lead, I did not have a roadmap. I did not wake up one day and say, "I know exactly how to become a leader." In fact, there were plenty of times I felt stuck, questioning if I was even on the right path. But here's what I learned along the way: you don't need to have it all figured out to move forward.

Direction is not about having a perfect plan. It's about having a purpose and trusting that the steps you take will lead you closer to where you're meant to be.

What Does "Finding Direction" Even Mean?

Finding direction is less about a specific destination and more about choosing a path that feels aligned with who you are. Think of it like hiking. You may not see the whole trail from the starting point, but as long as you know the direction you want to head, you will figure it out one step at a time. Leadership works the same way. The key is not seeing the end of the road; it's having the courage to take the first step.

Why Do We Struggle with Direction?

Let's talk about the roadblocks. Finding direction is not easy, and if you feel stuck, you're not alone. It is natural to struggle with direction. Sometimes direction seems to be this abstract concept that is not definable nor obtainable. Direction is not as obvious as it seems. Sometimes we have to start the journey before we know exactly where we are going. Many times, in your career, you will not know the exact end result, but you will continue anyway. That is direction. Direction is about creating momentum to where we eventually want to be. This can be devastating if we are not careful in making course corrections as we advance in our journey. I have friends who are pilots, and they remind me that an airplane is flying off course 98% of the time. The pilots are constantly adjusting for course corrections and weather and other challenges in the air, but they maintain a true compass that guarantees they will reach their intended destination. We must always be diligent in paying attention to our direction. Here are some common challenges:

We Overthink Everything

"What if I fail?" "What if I'm not good enough?" Stop. You don't have to know every answer right now. Move first; clarity will follow.

We're Paralyzed by Comparison

Someone else's journey is not yours. Stop measuring your progress against their highlight reel. Focus on your growth.

We Wait for Permission

Nobody's coming to anoint you as "ready." Step up, claim your role, and lead.

We Forget That Direction Changes

You're allowed to change your mind. As long as you're learning and growing, you're still moving in the right direction.

How Do You Overcome These Obstacles?

By staying grounded in your values, connected to your sense of purpose, and clear about who you are and what drives you, these guideposts help you stay on course even when the destination is not entirely clear.

In leadership—and in life—there's one question you have to keep asking yourself: "Where am I going?" Without a clear direction, even your hardest work won't yield meaningful results. Activity doesn't equal progress. You can be running full speed, but if you're heading the wrong way, you're just getting lost faster.

Actor Denzel Washington put it perfectly: "Don't

just aspire to make a living, aspire to make a difference. Just because you are doing a lot more doesn't mean you are getting a lot done. Don't confuse movement with progress. If it's not in the right direction, it's useless."

Direction is the foundation of being significant—it is the first of the Five Simple Truths. It gives clarity and purpose to your actions, helping you ensure that every step aligns with your ultimate goal(s). It is not about seeking titles as directional goals. This is one of the most critical mistakes people make when trying to determine direction. Only to find that the title never creates direction, it only creates more of an expectation of having clear direction.

So, take a moment to reflect. Are you moving with purpose, or just moving? Are your values and goals steering your path? When you lead with direction, you don't just make progress—you make a difference.

As Lao Tzu wisely said, "If you do not change direction, you may end up where you are heading." And that's what I have seen countless times in my career as a leader—people drifting through their jobs, frustrated because they never feel like they're getting anywhere. The truth is, if you don't intentionally set your course, you may end up far from where you intended. This is not just a problem for individuals, but for teams and organizations as well.

Vision: The Foundation of True Direction

Let's start simple—what is vision and why? Vision supports direction. For many, it might feel like some abstract, elusive concept reserved for the Steve Jobs or Winston Churchills of the world. But here is the truth: vision is simply the ability to see where you want to go and the commitment to stay true to your beliefs and values along the way. It is simpler than you think; it can start with just wanting to be a better leader, that is vision. It's the future state of things. Vision gives life to your direction.

Vision doesn't have to be grand or complicated. It starts with knowing what matters to you—your values —and using those as a compass for your decisions. Whether you're planning your day, your career, or your leadership legacy, without vision, leaders lose focus, and the people they lead become aimless, disengaged, and uncertain. Vision is the North Star that anchors your direction, even when life throws many storms your way.

A great leader is not just focused on what's in front of them—they can see beyond the daily grind to the bigger picture. They recognize the long-term goals and use them to inspire action and progress. Without vision, there's no clarity, and without clarity, your direction falters.

For me, vision was never about chasing perfection— it was about progress and creating a path. My personal vision was simple: "Be better today than I was yesterday." It did not matter how much I'd accomplished; I kept striving to improve. That's vision—a personal guidance system that aligns your actions with a higher purpose and steers your direction toward growth. This sustained me in so many tough moments.

How Vision Helps Direction

When I was a young police officer, I decided early on in my career that I wanted to one day be the Police Chief. I had no idea how I would make this happen or if I could, but I clearly began focusing on my vision. This created direction. I enrolled in college and began studying. I started journaling and keeping notes of my progress. Before I knew it, a direction unfolded. It became clear that I was going to have to push myself way out of my comfort zone and begin to make hard decisions. It meant me leaving an organization that I loved to take advantage of better promotional opportunities. It made my direction clear. Direction is so important and is guided by vision. Vision acts as the guiding light that defines **where** an organization, a team, or an individual is heading. Without vision, direction becomes reactive rather than intentional. **Leaders don't just respond to circumstances—they shape the future by setting a course.**

How Do You Find Direction When You're Not Sure Where to Go?

Look Inward Before You Look Outward

The first step to finding direction is understanding yourself. What do you value? What fires you up? What do you want your leadership to stand for? For me, it was integrity and service. I did not know how far I could go in law enforcement, but I knew I wanted to make a difference for my community. That clarity was my anchor.

Pick a General Destination

You don't need to map out every twist and turn. Just decide what you want to aim for. Do you want to be a leader others look up to? Someone who builds teams that thrive? Start with that. The details will come as you move.

Act, Even If It's Messy

Waiting for the perfect opportunity will keep you stuck forever. Volunteer for the tough projects, step into roles that scare you a little, and learn as you go. Leadership is not about getting it right every time; it's about showing up and growing through the process.

Don't Be Afraid to Pivot

The path you start on might not be the one you end on —and that's okay. Every step teaches you something about what you want and where you're meant to go.

Having clear direction doesn't mean you won't encounter obstacles. Following your vision will create many obstacles and hardships. In fact, it's during these moments of challenge that your direction becomes even more critical. When your ship is taking horrible winds and waves, it is really hard to stay the course. Staying focused on your vision will calm those obstacles. It keeps you steady when the winds blow the hardest.

Personal Direction vs. Organizational Direction

As a leader, it's not enough to have direction for yourself; you must also be able to articulate that direction to those around you. Whether you're leading a small team or a large organization, direction is the difference between a motivated workforce and a disengaged one. People need to understand the 'why' behind what they do. If they know where they're going and why it matters, they're far more likely to invest in the journey. People are most productive when they are following both personal and organizational vision. It creates a sense of direction that creates motivation.

Consider Steve Jobs and his direction for Apple. Jobs' vision for Apple was not just to make computers, but to make a dent in the universe. He did not settle for mediocrity, and because of his clear vision, he rallied his team to push boundaries, innovate, and strive for excellence. When you have a clear direction, others will follow you with enthusiasm because they can see the destination and understand their role in reaching it.

One exercise that can help is visualizing where you want to be in five years. Imagine the life you want, the impact you have made, and the leadership role you have cultivated. From there, work backward to today and ask, "What do I need to do now to get there?"

Direction in Action: The Case of Nelson Mandela

Few leaders understood the importance of direction as deeply as Nelson Mandela. Imprisoned for 27 years, Mandela never lost sight of his ultimate goal: a free and equal South Africa. Even when he was isolated from the world, Mandela's direction remained unshaken. His leadership did not waver because he was clear on his purpose and vision for his country. When he was finally released and became South Africa's first Black president, Mandela's direction led not only to his personal success, but the liberation of a nation.

This story demonstrates a critical point: having direction is not just about guiding yourself; it's about *inspiring* others to follow you on a shared journey. Mandela's unyielding direction inspired millions to believe in the possibility of a better future, and it's what gave him the fortitude to endure years of hardship.

HOW DIRECTION RELATES TO THE FIVE SIMPLE TRUTHS

Intentionality: Once direction is set, intentionality becomes crucial. Purposeful actions follow naturally when you have a clear understanding of where you're heading. Leaders can waste a lot of energy on well-meaning actions that don't align with the ultimate goal, but intentionality ensures every decision supports the larger mission.

Teams: Clear direction enhances team dynamics. When everyone knows the direction, each member of the team can align their efforts to reach common objectives. It's much easier for people to work together effectively when they know what they're working toward and how their role contributes.

Standards: Direction sets the benchmarks for success. Standards flow from understanding where you need to go. When you have clear direction, it's easier to define the level of excellence required. A team without direction lacks clear standards, which leads to inconsistency and confusion.

Getting Ahead of Your Day: To truly get ahead of your day, you need to start with a sense of direction. Knowing where you're going lets you prioritize what needs to be accomplished each day. Without direction, it's easy to get bogged down in tasks that don't matter, and you will spend more time reacting instead of leading.

Practical Tips for Creating a System to Establishing Your Direction

- Define Your Vision: What do you want tomorrow to look like? Get clear on where you want to go. Write it down, visualize it, and let it guide your decision-making process.
- Break it Down: Once you have a vision, break it down into smaller, actionable goals. What can you do today, this week, or this month to get closer to heading in that direction?
- Communicate It: Share your direction with those around you—your team, your family, your mentors. Create an expectation of accountability by naming your direction and where you are heading. When others know your direction, they can help you stay on course.
- Stay Flexible, but Focused: Direction is not a rigid path. Many times, the route may change, but your ultimate goal should remain steadfast.
- Start: Don't wait for the perfect plan or strategy. See it and you can do it.

Direction is the first Simple Truth because without it, none of the others matter. You can work hard, be intentional, and have high standards, but if you're headed in the wrong direction, none of that will lead you to becoming significant. When you have Direction, everything you do becomes purposeful.

"

Intentionality is putting action into thoughts. We have thousands and thousands of thoughts a day. If we don't become intentional regarding those thoughts, they stay trapped. Intentionality frees our thoughts from the confines of our minds.

Chapter 2
Intentionality: The Second Simple Truth

IN THE FAST-PACED WORLD WE LIVE IN, IT'S easy to get caught up in the whirlwind of activity without ever stopping to ask, "Is this getting me closer to where I want to be?" "Am I getting closer to what I need to be doing to make me the best leader possible?" Questions like these are examples of why the second simple truth—Intentionality—is so crucial. Intentionality is about acting with purpose and making deliberate choices that align with your direction. The law of intentionality is simple: "What you tend to set your mind to gets done." This is a truth that cannot be understated. Simple acts of intentionality on a consistent basis can improve your results dramatically.

One of the most dangerous traps leaders fall into is busyness. You might think that by staying busy, you're being productive, but in reality, busy work is often the enemy of progress. As the legendary Stoic philosopher Seneca said, "We suffer more often in imagination than in reality." In leadership, the same holds true: we often fill our time with tasks that seem urgent but have little bearing on our actual success. Intentionality demands that you stop, think, and make decisions based on where you want to go. Intentionality is putting action into thoughts. We have thousands and thousands of thoughts a day. If we don't become intentional regarding those thoughts, they stay trapped. Intentionality frees our thoughts from the confines of our minds.

The Power of Focused Intentionality

One of the best examples of intentional leadership comes from General Dwight D. Eisenhower. During World War II, Eisenhower was tasked with planning and executing the D-Day invasion, one of the most complex military operations in history. The success of the operation was not a result of last-minute scrambling or scattered decision-making; it was the product of focused and intentional planning.

Eisenhower understood that every decision, every allocation of resources, every order given had to be intentional. There was no room for second-guessing or indecision. His intentional leadership led to the successful invasion of Normandy, which ultimately contributed to the defeat of Nazi Germany.

Intentionality vs. Reactivity

There's a big difference between being intentional and being reactive. When you're reactive, you're always at the mercy of external forces—other people's priorities, the latest crisis, or the demands of the moment. In contrast, being intentional means that you take control of your actions and decisions.

Abraham Lincoln once said, "Give me six hours to chop down a tree and I will spend the first four sharpening the axe." This quote perfectly illustrates the principle of intentionality. Too many leaders jump into action without sharpening their axes—without taking the time to plan and act with purpose.

When you're intentional, you don't just "chop at the tree" mindlessly. You step back, assess the situation, and make strategic choices. This applies to all aspects of leadership, from how you manage your time to how you communicate with your team.

Intentional Leaders Create Momentum

Momentum creates sustained action that leads to results. Leaders who want to move themselves and the organization in the right direction need positive momentum to accomplish that goal. Another great example of intentionality in action is General Colin Powell. Powell, who served as the U.S. Secretary of State and a four-star general, was known for his deliberate and thoughtful leadership style. He once said, "There are no secrets to success. It is the result of preparation, hard work, and learning from failure." Powell's approach was rooted in intentionality. He believed that success wasn't about luck but about consistently applying effort in the right direction. This creates momentum.

This kind of intentionality builds momentum over time. When you consistently make decisions aligned with your goals, you start to see the results compound. Suddenly, you're not just moving toward success— you're accelerating toward it. Intentional leaders know that every choice, no matter how small, either pushes them closer to or further away from their goals.

Psychologist Peter Gollwitzer introduced the idea of implementation intention to make it easier to act on your goals. In other words: be more intentional. The concept is simple: create a specific plan that connects a future situation with a specific action.

It works like this: "If X happens, then I will do Y."

Implementation of intentions transforms vague goals into clear plans of action. Instead of relying on motivation alone, you prepare your brain and environment to support you when it's time to act.

This plan pre-decides your action in response to a situation, making it easier to follow through because you have already mapped out what to do when the moment arises. If you create an intentional action, let's say getting up at a certain time every morning and working out, this predetermines in your mind that this time is set aside to work out. For example, "If it's 8 a.m., then I will go for a run." This strategy turns vague intentions into clear, actionable steps, making it much more likely you will follow through. Scheduling acts of intentionality can help you put them into action. Realizing that procrastination is also the act of being intentional. Scheduling the time to do things and doing them can help thwart the desire to procrastinate. Let intentionality create the premise to follow through with direction.

Intentionality in Leadership: The Case of Satya Nadella

One of the most striking modern examples of intentional leadership is Satya Nadella, the CEO of Microsoft. When Nadella took the helm in 2014, Microsoft was facing significant challenges. Once a dominant force in the tech world, the company had lost ground to competitors like Apple, Google, and Amazon. Microsoft needed a leader who could guide it back to relevance, and Nadella rose to the occasion with intentionality at the core of his approach.

From day one, Nadella made deliberate choices that aligned with his vision for the company. He shifted Microsoft's focus from being a "know-it-all" culture to a "learn-it-all" culture. This was not a reactive decision but a purposeful move to foster innovation and collaboration within the organization. Nadella's intentionality extended beyond cultural shifts. He made strategic investments in cloud computing, recognizing that it was the future of technology. Under his leadership, Microsoft Azure became a central pillar of the company's success, allowing it to compete directly with Amazon Web Services and Google Cloud.

Nadella also chose to repair relationships with former rivals. For years, Microsoft had been known for its aggressive competition with companies like Apple and open-source communities. Nadella intentionally shifted this stance, forging partnerships that had previously seemed impossible. This was a calculated move to align the company with its long-term goals of growth and adaptability.

What makes Nadella's story so impactful is not just the success Microsoft achieved under his leadership, but the intentionality behind every step he took. He did not allow immediate pressures or past failures to dictate his actions. Instead, he acted with clear purpose, focusing on long-term success over short-term wins.

Nadella's leadership demonstrates that intentionality is about making choices with purpose and clarity. It's about understanding where you want to go and taking deliberate steps to get there. By focusing on what truly matters—whether that's innovation, culture, or collaboration—leaders can create momentum that drives sustained success.

Procrastination is intentional, too, but it can lead to stagnation. Leaders like Nadella remind us that intentional action, rooted in a clear vision, is what moves organizations forward. As a leader, you have the power to create change, but only if you're willing to act with purpose, even when the path is challenging.

The Ripple Effect of Intentionality

Intentionality doesn't just impact your own leadership journey—it shapes the very culture around you. When a leader acts with clear purpose, it sends a ripple through their organization. Teams begin to mirror that same focus. Decisions become sharper. Meetings become more productive. Projects gain speed and clarity. It's like a tuning fork: the leader strikes the note, and everyone else tunes to that frequency.

On the flip side, a lack of intentionality creates confusion. People don't know what matters. Priorities shift like sand. Energy gets wasted. Morale suffers. In the absence of clear, deliberate leadership, mediocrity moves in like an uninvited guest and overstays its welcome.

Intentional leadership either builds an organization—or its absence dismantles it one decision at a time.

Why Most Leaders Fail at Intentionality

It's not because they don't care. It's because they don't slow down.

They get caught in the buzzsaw of daily operations, constantly reacting, constantly putting out fires, and before they know it, they have lost sight of the mission. Their days are full, but their impact is thin.

It takes real courage to say, "I'm not going to get swept away by today's noise. I'm going to focus on what moves the needle."

Intentionality is not about perfection—it's about consistency. It's not a once-a-year leadership retreat buzzword; it's a daily discipline.

Every morning when you lace up your boots as a leader, you make a choice:

Will today be dictated by chance?

Or will it be driven by purpose?

The Power of Intentional Questions

One practical way to stay anchored in intentionality is to ask powerful daily questions.

Consider ending your day by asking yourself:

- "Did my actions today move me closer to my mission?"
- "What did I say yes to that I shouldn't't have?"
- "Where did I spend energy that did not align with my priorities?"
- "What one thing can I do tomorrow with greater intentionality?"

Questions like these create what psychologists call a "reflexive pause"—a moment where you interrupt the autopilot mode and reassert control over your direction.

A Final Word: The Legacy of Intentional Leaders

In the end, intentionality is about legacy. The question isn't just "What am I achieving today?" but "What am I building for tomorrow?"

The leaders we remember—the ones who change industries, nations, or lives—were not the busiest leaders. They were the ones who acted **on purpose, with purpose, for a purpose.**

Becoming an intentional leader does not mean every day is perfect or that every plan works out exactly as designed. It means you refuse to leave your leadership to chance. It means you choose clarity over chaos, discipline over drift, and progress over distraction.

Intentionality is the slow, steady drumbeat that creates extraordinary leadership.

It is how ordinary people build extraordinary legacies.

How Intentionality Relates to the Five Simple Truths

Direction: Intentionality stems from having a clear direction. If you know where you're going, you can act purposefully to reach that destination. A leader who lacks direction might be busy, but their actions lack purpose. Intentionality ensures every effort contributes to the end goal.

Teams: Teams operate best when their efforts are intentional and focused on a shared goal. By setting a clear intention, leaders foster a team dynamic where every member understands their purpose and works toward the collective mission.

Standards: Acting with intention requires high standards. It's not enough to just "do;" leaders must set the bar high and ensure their actions and the actions of their teams meet the expected level of excellence. Intentionality keeps leaders from settling for mediocrity.

Getting Ahead of Your Day: Intentionality enables you to structure your day with purpose. Knowing what needs to be done and acting with purpose helps you stay ahead. Every moment spent without intentional focus is time lost reacting to circumstances rather than controlling them.

Practical Steps to Becoming More Intentional

- Identify Your Priorities: Start by defining what's most important to you. What are the top three things you need to focus on to achieve your goals? Write them down and revisit them often.

- Say No to Distractions: One of the hardest but most important parts of being intentional is learning to say no. Every time you say yes to something that doesn't align with your priorities, you're taking time and energy away from what truly matters.
- Focus on High-Impact Activities: Not all tasks are created equal. Identify the activities that will have the greatest impact on your goals, and focus your energy on those.
- Set Clear Boundaries: Being intentional often means setting boundaries around your time and energy. Make sure that you're allocating your resources in a way that aligns with your goals.
- Reflect Regularly: Take time to reflect on your progress and reassess your direction. Are your actions still aligned with your goals? If not, it's time to recalibrate. Conclusion: Direction + Intentionality = Progress

Intentionality is the bridge between ambition and achievement. It turns lofty goals into tangible outcomes and ensures that every step you take leads you closer to your vision.

When combined with a clear direction,

Intentionality builds momentum, creating a cycle of success that fuels itself. Leaders who act with Intentionality inspire others, foster trust, and leave a lasting impact.

"

Teams are not just groups of people
working together—they are the engines of
collaboration, innovation, and resilience. A
strong team supports each other, pushes
through challenges, and rallies around a
common purpose. When teams falter, so
does the mission.

Chapter 3
Teams: The Third Simple Truth

LEADERSHIP IS NEVER A SOLO ENDEAVOR. While stories of individual brilliance often capture our imagination, the truth is that no significant achievement happens in isolation. Behind every great leader is a team—a collective force driving the mission forward. Teams amplify the leader's vision, provide diverse perspectives, and turn plans into action. Without them, even the most determined leader will fall short of their potential.

Building and sustaining effective teams, however, remains one of the most challenging aspects of leadership. Reflecting on my own journey, many of my leadership struggles were rooted in two critical issues: either I did not have the right team in place, or I failed to fully develop and unlock the potential of the team. Building effective teams can prove to be very challenging, but it will be worth every minute you spend.

This chapter explores the third fundamental truth of

leadership: the power of teams. Not just any teams, but the specific types of teams that are critical for leadership success. Let's dive into how to identify, build, and strengthen these teams to achieve extraordinary results.

Why Teams Are So Important

Teams are not just groups of people working together—they are the engines of collaboration, innovation, and resilience. A strong team supports each other, pushes through challenges, and rallies around a common purpose. When teams falter, so does the mission.

One of the most pressing challenges leaders face today is dealing with problem employees or difficult team members. These individuals may resist standards, disengage, or create friction within the group. I have found a common root cause for problem employees is that they have lost their sense of belonging to the team. They no longer see themselves as part of a collective effort; they have become, in essence, a "team of none." Just like a bad apple, one bad team member can spoil the entire basket.

Their loss of connection or belief —whether to their peers, the mission, or the organization—can have a cascading effect. When employees lose belief in themselves or the team, their performance suffers and morale declines. It is a leader's responsibility to recognize these fractures early and address them head-on. Leaders have to focus on the three types of teams and navigate the employees through these teams in order to make long-lasting changes to their behavior. A common mistake I made early on in my career was thinking I could skip from a Team of One to a Team of We with employees. This never worked for the long term. I may get quick compliance due to an energized, renewed belief in themselves to see the bigger picture of what we were trying to accomplish, but without seeing the importance of a Team of Two, they had difficulty in working with others. This defeated the work we had done.

Three Types of Teams: One, Two, and We

Building Teams: From One to We

Leadership is fundamentally about building teams, but the process doesn't begin by focusing on the entire group. Effective leadership starts with an inward focus and then grows outward in intentional layers. To truly lead and inspire others, you must understand and culti-vate three essential types of teams: Team of One, Team of Two, and Team of We. These layers represent a progression, where each one builds upon the previous. Neglecting any one layer undermines the foundation of the others. It is vital to get employees that you are working with to include problem employees to focus on this concept. No one can possibly be a Team of Two or a Team of We without first being a Team of One.

Team of One: Mastering Self-Leadership

The journey to building great teams begins with a Team of One—yourself. Before you can effectively lead others, you must first lead yourself. This means cultivating self-discipline, accountability, and the drive to achieve personal excellence. A leader who lacks self-awareness or personal accountability will struggle to inspire confidence and trust in their team.

Imagine a leader who is disorganized, reactive, or inconsistent. Their team will mirror those same qualities. By contrast, a leader who consistently demonstrates focus, discipline, and intentionality sets the tone for the entire organization. This concept is best exemplified by the Japanese term *kaizen,* which means continuous self-improvement. Great leaders are always striving to be the best version of themselves because they understand that their personal habits and mindset will ripple outward.

Consider Marcus Aurelius, the Stoic philosopher and Roman Emperor. Despite the immense pressures of ruling an empire, he consistently practiced self-discipline and journaling daily to reflect on his values and decisions. His ability to lead himself first set the foundation for his ability to lead others effectively.

How to Build Your Team of One:

1. Develop Daily Habits: Whether it's journaling, exercising, or planning your day, consistent habits build discipline.
2. Hold Yourself Accountable: Set measurable goals and regularly evaluate your progress.
3. Lead by Example: Display the work ethic, integrity, and standards you expect from others.

Team of Two: The Power of Partnership

Once you have mastered the Team of One, the next step is forming a Team of Two—a partnership. This is the bridge between personal accountability and broader collaboration. A Team of Two fosters mutual support, shared accountability, and a sense of partnership that drives collective effort.

Consider a leader paired with a trusted lieutenant, mentor, or colleague. Together, they amplify each other's strengths and balance each other's weaknesses. A Team of Two provides a safe space for honest feedback, encouragement, and shared problem-solving. It also creates an accountability loop: when you know someone else is depending on you, you're more likely to stay committed to your goals.

Take, for example, the story of Ruth Bader Ginsburg and her husband, Marty Ginsburg. Throughout their lives, they supported each other's ambitions while maintaining their own individual identities. Ruth's rise to become a Supreme Court Justice was supported by Marty's encouragement, advocacy, and belief in her abilities. Together, they exemplified the power of a Team of Two.

Why it Matters

A Team of Two creates synergy—where the whole is greater than the sum of its parts. This dynamic is especially powerful in leadership because it reinforces commitment and shared purpose.

Committing to Service in a Team of Two

Committing to service means putting a mission above personal comfort, choosing responsibility over convenience, and embracing the mindset that leadership is about contribution, not recognition. In a Team of Two, this commitment is amplified—each person becomes accountable not just to themselves, but to their partner and the greater purpose they serve. True service requires sacrifice; it means setting aside ego, pushing beyond limits, and focusing on solutions rather than obstacles. When two people commit to service together, they create a force that drives excellence, inspires others, and ensures that challenges are met with determination, not defeat. A Team of Two doesn't just share the workload—they share the responsibility to lead, serve, and make a difference.

Think of an exercise partner. On days when you're tempted to skip the gym, the knowledge that someone else is counting on you motivates you to show up. This principle works just as well in professional settings.

Examples of a Team of Two

- Mentor and Mentee: The mentor provides guidance and wisdom, while the mentee brings fresh perspectives and energy. Both grow from the relationship.
- Command Staff Relationship: A Chief and Deputy Chief who communicate openly, support each other, and share the mission's vision can drive an entire department forward.
- Workout Partner: Workout partners hold each other accountable by making sure they show up to the gym. They also make sure that they push each other to get the maximum effort from each other.
- Supervisor and Problem Employee: Problem employees can benefit from a supervisor who is willing to help them and guide them along the improvement process. This creates buy in from both parties and success is more likely.

How to Build Your Team of Two

1. Establish Clear Goals: Define what success looks like for both of you.
2. Communicate Often: Regular, honest conversations build trust and alignment.
3. Support Each Other's Growth: Celebrate wins, provide feedback, and be there during setbacks.
4. Create belief in something that you can work together on that requires supporting each other.
5. Hold each other accountable.

Team of We: Collective Leadership

The ultimate goal is to build a Team of We, where the focus expands to include everyone in your organization, group, or mission. A Team of We is not limited to the people that may be on your smaller team within the organization. It harnesses the collective power of the entire group, aligning individual strengths toward a shared purpose. It's no longer about individual goals or even small partnerships; it's about creating a total culture where everyone feels ownership and responsibility for the bigger team's success.

However, this larger team can only succeed if the foundational layers—Team of One and Team of Two—are strong. Many leaders make the mistake of focusing solely on the big picture without addressing individual accountability or partnerships first. This creates teams that are fragmented, directionless, or overly reliant on the leader to solve every problem.

Building a Team of We requires a shared vision, clear communication, and a culture of trust. Leaders who focus on collaboration rather than hierarchy foster a sense of collective ownership. This doesn't mean everyone agrees on everything; it means everyone is committed to the team's success despite differences.

A Team of We achieves what no individual or small group could accomplish alone. However, this level of teamwork only thrives when the foundation—strong Teams of One and Two—is in place. Without personal accountability and trust-based partnerships, larger teams often collapse under miscommunication and conflicting priorities. By being a part of the Team of We, you create self-drive and stay motivated for the bigger purpose.

Team of We – The Success of SpaceX's Falcon 9 Reusability Program

An example of a Team of We comes from SpaceX and their groundbreaking work in rocket reusability, particularly with the Falcon 9 program. This achievement wasn't the result of a single genius or even a small leadership team—it required the collaboration, dedication, and alignment of thousands of individuals working toward a shared vision.

When Elon Musk and SpaceX set out to create

reusable rockets, the goal wasn't just ambitious—it was transformative. Rocket reusability had been dismissed for decades as impractical due to the extreme challenges involved. It required innovations across multiple disciplines: engineering, software development, manufacturing, and operations. Each team had to push the limits of their expertise, knowing that even a minor error could jeopardize the mission.

Despite these challenges, SpaceX achieved its first successful Falcon 9 booster landing in 2015, a feat that fundamentally changed the aerospace industry by drastically reducing launch costs. This historic moment was made possible by a Team of We.

How To Build Your Team of We

1. Shared Vision: Every employee needs to be aligned with a common mission. This larger purpose unites everyone, from top-level to assembly line workers.

2. Collaboration Across Disciplines: Success depends on close collaboration between teams with different specialties. Each team understands how their role contributes to the bigger picture, ensuring seamless integration of efforts.

3. Clear Communication: To function effectively as a Team of We, leaders must foster open communication at all levels. Teams share

ideas, lessons learned, and progress updates, ensuring alignment and minimizing silos. Emphasize transparency and cross-department collaboration, breaking down barriers that often hinder innovation in large organizations.

4. High Standards: Operate with the highest performance standards. Everyone should know that excellence is non-negotiable. Everyone is held to the same high expectations because the stakes are too high for mediocrity.

5. Resilience in Failure: Failure is absolute in every company. You will face significant setbacks, instead of assigning blame, the company treats failures as collective learning opportunities. This resilience strengthens their culture as a Team of We and ensures continual improvement.

Great leadership is not about individual brilliance; it's about uniting people around a common goal, empowering them to contribute their best, and fostering an environment where collaboration and innovation thrive. In today's interconnected and complex world, the Team of We model is more relevant than ever. It's how extraordinary results are achieved.

Moving Through the Layers

The progression from Team of One to Team of Two to Team of We is not linear; it's dynamic and iterative. Each layer reinforces the others. A strong (Team of One) ensures that you bring discipline and focus to partnerships (Team of Two). Effective partnerships then help you build credibility and trust to lead larger groups (Team of We).

For example, consider the leadership of Serena Williams. As an individual athlete, she exemplified the (Team of One) by maintaining extraordinary focus and discipline. In her partnership with her coach and family (Team of Two), she found the support and accountability necessary to sustain her career. Finally, in representing her sport and advocating for equality, she became a part of the larger Team of We, inspiring change across the tennis community and beyond.

The Big Picture

Building effective teams is a layered process:

- Start with One by mastering self-leadership.
- Expand to Two by forming strong partnerships built on trust and shared goals.
- Grow into We by leading and inspiring a collective team to achieve something greater.

Why Teams Matter in Leadership

Teams amplify the abilities of individual leaders. A leader's vision, no matter how compelling, is meaningless without a team to bring it to life. Teams also provide diverse perspectives, shared workload, and resilience in the face of challenges.

Teams matter because they create a sense of belonging and purpose. When people feel they are part of something bigger than themselves, they are more likely to be engaged, motivated, and committed to excellence.

How Teams Relates to the Five Simple Truths

Direction: Teams need clear direction to succeed. Leaders must communicate the "why" behind their vision, aligning individual efforts with organizational goals.

Intentionality: Building and nurturing teams requires intentionality. Every action a leader takes, from hiring decisions to team meetings, should serve to strengthen the team.

Standards: High-performing teams operate with clear standards. Leaders set the tone by defining expectations and holding everyone accountable to them.

Getting Ahead of Your Day: Teams that anticipate challenges and plan ahead are more effective. A proactive team leader fosters a culture where preparation is a shared responsibility.

Practical Action Steps to Build Effective Teams

- Start with Yourself: Cultivate self-discipline, accountability, and personal growth. Be a Team of One that others can rely on.
- Foster Strong Partnerships: Build meaningful one-on-one relationships that support mutual growth and accountability.
- Create a Collective Vision: Align your team around a shared mission. Make sure every member understands how their role contributes to the larger goal.
- Establish Clear Standards: Define what success looks like for your team and ensure everyone is committed to those standards.
- Invest in Team Development: Provide resources, training, and opportunities for growth. Strong teams are built, not born.

The simple truth of Teams reminds us that leadership is never a solo journey. Whether it's leading yourself, partnering with others, or guiding a larger organization, the power of Teams is indispensable.

Teams are where leadership comes alive—where vision becomes action, and action becomes achievement. But Teams don't just happen. They require effort, intentionality, and a commitment to building relationships at every level.

"

Expectations and standards are not
the same, yet they are often treated as
interchangeable. Expectations define what
needs to be done, while standards define
how well it should be done. When we fail
to clearly communicate the standard, we
leave a significant gap that undermines
performance and accountability.

Chapter 4
Having High Standards: The Fourth Simple Truth

HAVING HIGH STANDARDS IS THE KEY TO HIGH performance. I have done many things in my life like most of you, but when I hold myself to the highest standards, I accomplish the most. When you hold yourself to high standards, you will always like the results. In leadership, it is easy to talk about having standards. But, as with most things in life, the real challenge lies in holding yourself and others to those standards consistently. The fourth Simple Truth is all about setting the bar for excellence—and beyond.

The Power of Standards in Leadership: Beyond Expectations

As a leader, I have often been told—and I have long believed—that setting clear expectations is the foundation of creating performance, motivation, and results. And there's a certain truth in that. Expectations give people a framework to understand their roles and responsibilities, providing direction for their efforts. But I have found there is more than setting expectations to get the most out of ourselves and others.

Over the years, I have filled out countless performance evaluations for employees and received many myself. These evaluations serve a purpose: they communicate expectations and offer a structure for accountability.

However, what is frequently missing from performance evaluations—and from leadership communication in general—is a critical piece of the puzzle: the level of standard at which we expect those expectations to be met. It is far more than establishing a numerical rating of one to five as it relates to standards.

Expectations vs. Standards

Expectations and standards are not the same, yet they are often treated as interchangeable. Expectations define what needs to be done, while standards define how well it should be done. When we fail to clearly communicate the standard, we leave a significant gap that undermines performance and accountability.

Imagine telling someone to "complete a project by the end of the week" but neglecting to explain the quality of work you're looking for. Does "complete" mean finishing it at a satisfactory level, or does it mean producing something exceptional that reflects excellence? Without setting the standard, you leave room for misinterpretation—and ultimately, mediocrity. I have made this simple but powerful error of assuming that the employee understands the standards in which to complete the task. The result is often misaligned with what I expect and what they deliver, resulting in frustration and loss of time for the leader, employee, and ultimately for the organization.

Performance Evaluations: A Missed Opportunity

Traditional performance evaluations often reinforce a disconnect. They typically assign numerical ratings—say, on a scale from one to five—to correlate with performance. While these numbers offer a way to quantify results, they rarely communicate the significance of the standard attached to the performance.

Let's say an employee receives a "3" on their evaluation, indicating they have met expectations. But what does that really mean? Did they meet the expectations at a "good enough" level, or did they meet them with excellence? The absence of clarity around standards limits the ability to inspire greater effort or guide improvement. There are multiple tasks that need to be performed at a very high level. As leaders, we must make it a habit to articulate not just what we expect, but the level of excellence we expect. Without this, we're only sharing half the equation.

The Importance of Standards

Standards are the benchmarks that guide individuals and teams toward greatness. They define the "why" and the "how" behind our expectations. Leaders who fail to set clear standards risk creating environments where "just getting by" becomes the norm.

Consider this quote from Vince Lombardi: "Perfection is not attainable, but if we chase perfection, we can catch excellence." Lombardi's words underscore the importance of high standards. When leaders set the bar high and communicate those expectations effectively, they inspire teams to stretch beyond their perceived limits. Standards shape the culture of an organization, driving motivation and aligning individual efforts with collective goals.

Communicating Standards Alongside Expectations

When explaining an expectation, leaders must also define the accompanying standard. Here is an example:

Expectation: "Submit the project report by Friday."

Standard: "Submit the report in a format that is detailed, error-free, and reflects thorough analysis along with a clear understanding of the bigger picture and how that impacts our ability to complete the project. I expect your best effort and if you have further questions, please let me know."

I guarantee this will produce a much better report than simply saying, "Get it done."

By pairing the expectation with the standard, you eliminate ambiguity and set the stage for accountability. This approach ensures that team members understand not just what they need to do, but how well they need to do it.

The Role of Standards in Motivation

Clear standards are not just about performance—they also play a crucial role in motivation. People are naturally more engaged and driven when they understand the importance of their work and how it contributes to a larger vision. Setting high standards signals that their efforts matter and that excellence is valued.

The famous architect Frank Lloyd Wright once said: "The thing always happens that you really believe in; and the belief in a thing makes it happen." When leaders believe in the power of high standards and communicate them with conviction, they instill that same belief in their teams. This belief becomes the foundation for motivation, driving people to go above and beyond.

Leadership is not just about telling people what to do; it's about inspiring them to do it well. By pairing clear expectations with high standards, leaders set the stage for meaningful performance and sustained success.

Remember, expectations outline the destination, but standards define the journey. Leaders who focus on both create environments where excellence thrives, and teams consistently achieve more than they thought possible. We should always explain the standard with the expectation.

Five Key Standards of Performance

There are five key standards you need to understand: **Poor, Average, Good, Excellent, and Elite**. These standards represent more than performance levels— they reflect the mindset of the individuals who hold them. As a leader, understanding where your team members stand on this spectrum is essential, because it helps you identify who needs external motivation and who can drive themselves towards success.

Before diving into each of these standards, let's set the stage: Self-drive is so important as a leadership trait. Those who hold themselves to higher standards— Excellent or Elite—tend to be internally motivated and self-driven. They don't need a constant push to perform; they thrive on their own desire for growth and success. In contrast, those with Poor, Average, or even Good standards often rely on external motivation to get things done. I have known many successful leaders and people in my life. The most successful ones hold themselves to the highest of standards.

Let's explore each of these standards in depth: Imagine using a bell shape curve to compare standards and performance. We have all seen a bell shape curve. It is used as a distribution of what you are measuring. In this case, we are measuring standards. At the far right, you have people who hold themselves to an Elite standard and at the far left, you have people who hold themselves to a Poor standard. Now let's explain how this distribution works.

1. Poor

The Poor standard is where we find those at the bottom 10% of an organization. These individuals do the bare minimum to get by. They meet just enough of the requirements to stay employed but rarely push beyond that. Their attitude might be along the lines of, "It's good enough for now," or, "As long as I'm not getting fired, I'm fine."

Poor performers need constant external motivation and supervision. They lack the internal drive that leads to growth, and more often than not, they create problems for the organization. Their low standards not only hold them back but can also drag others down with them. As a leader, your goal is not necessarily to push Poor performers to Elite—the gap can be too wide—but rather than try to fix them or get them to be immediate top performers, attempt to raise their standards incrementally. One way is explaining why it starts with them seeing the value of having higher standards. Encourage them to see that being a good Team of One can result in benefits that are important not only to them, but the entire group.

Poor performers have lost their self-drive to perform at a higher rate. The reasons can be many but are often the result of organizational betrayal or failure of leaders to appropriately address issues in a timely fashion. Poor performers are monuments to poor supervisors. Remember, as a leader, "If you permit it, you promote it."

Example: Enron's Collapse

In the corporate scandal that was Enron, many employees operated under a Poor standard—taking shortcuts and cutting corners because the leadership allowed them to do so. It was all about individual rewards. Low standards and lack of integrity permeated the company from the top down, which eventually led to its downfall. This was one of the largest corporate failures in U.S. history.

2. Average

The Average standard represents the middle of the road. Unfortunately, but also necessary to the organizational needs, these employees make up the bulk of most organizations (about 30%-50%). They show up, do their job competently, and meet expectations, but they rarely exceed them. Average people don't create problems, but they don't necessarily solve them either. They do what is required, but not much more. Average standards are accepted by most organizations.

Employees who think that average standards are acceptable need extrinsic motivation to perform at their best. This type of motivation consists of tangible things. They might be driven by incentives like promotions or bonuses, but their intrinsic motivation is usually lacking. As a leader, your challenge is to inspire them to go from Average to Good—helping them see the value in doing more than what's required. Average employees have the potential to reach higher levels of performance if given the right motivation. The key is to create self-drive in the employees so that they can find their own motivation.

Example: Blockbuster's Decline

Blockbuster Video serves as a case study of an Average organization that failed to innovate. Some of you reading this book will remember going to Blockbuster with your parents to pick out movies you would watch. It was a cultural norm to rent movies and return them. While Netflix was pushing boundaries and thinking ahead, Blockbuster remained complacent, focused on doing "enough" to stay relevant without striving for excellence or innovation. Eventually, that mindset caught up with them.

3. Good

This is where we start to see higher levels of performance. People who hold themselves to a Good standard often possess natural talents or skills that allow them to succeed. They take pride in their work and generally meet high expectations. However, Good is often the ceiling for these individuals because they don't consistently push themselves to be better. They are comfortable being competent but lack significant self-drive to pursue greatness.

Many people at the Good level can easily slide into complacency. Without a push from leadership, they might stay here indefinitely. These are the people who tend to think, "If it's not broken, why fix it?" They need occasional motivation to strive for more, but unlike Poor or Average performers, they have the potential to move up to Excellent rather quickly with the right guidance. I have always heard Good is the enemy of Great. This is true with standards.

Quote from Marcus Aurelius: "The impediment to action advances action. What stands in the way becomes the way." For people at the Good standard, leadership should focus on helping them overcome obstacles, turning challenges into opportunities for growth.

Example: Imagine a sales team at a mid-sized technology company. This team consistently meets its quarterly sales targets and is known for providing decent customer service. The team members have a good understanding of the company's products and can competently address customer needs. Their leader rarely needs to intervene, as they hit the numbers and maintain solid relationships with clients.

This is the Good standard in action: reliable, consistent, and competent. However, it's also clear that the team is operating at a plateau. They're not actively seeking to expand their client base, improve processes, or exceed expectations.

4. Excellent

Now we're talking about the top 10% of performers—those who consistently go above and beyond. These are the people who don't need external motivation because they are driven by internal goals and standards. Excellent individuals understand that greatness requires effort, consistency, and commitment. They are the backbone of high-performing teams, setting an example for others to follow.

In the Excellent category, self-drive is key. People in this group are not satisfied with just doing a good job; they are constantly looking for ways to improve, grow, and challenge themselves. They push through obstacles and embrace continuous learning. As a leader, your goal with these individuals is to nurture their growth and provide them with opportunities to excel even further.

Example: General Patton's leadership style is a great example of someone who consistently demanded Excellence from his troops. He did not accept excuses and maintained incredibly high standards, which translated into one of the most effective fighting forces in WWII.

5. Elite

At the very top of the spectrum is the Elite standard—representing the top 1% of performers. These are the people who don't just meet expectations—they redefine them. They are trailblazers, innovators, and top-level performers who are always looking for the next challenge. Elite performers are self-motivated to an extreme degree. They don't need external rewards because the pursuit of mastery and success is their driving force. This level of performance is very difficult to sustain. It requires a constant state of discomfort and struggle, but it is necessary at times to be Elite. Imagine a surgeon performing a life-saving surgery. Elite standards are the only acceptable standard. No one wants a surgeon who holds themselves to an Average standard to be their doctor.

Elite leaders shape the culture and trajectory of entire organizations. They inspire those around them, set new benchmarks, and drive the collective performance of their teams. They don't just meet high standards; they create them. As a leader, your role with Elite performers is to give them room to innovate, challenge the status quo, and continue setting new goals.

Example: Elon Musk's leadership at SpaceX is an example of Elite performance. He did not just want to create a space exploration company—he wanted to revolutionize the industry. His Elite drive has pushed his teams to achieve things many believed were impossible.

Self-Drive: The Key to Leadership Success

As we have discussed, one of the fundamental differences between those who operate at Poor, Average, and Good levels versus those at Excellent and Elite is self-drive. People at the lower end of the spectrum need constant motivation from external sources. They require rewards, incentives, or even threats of consequences to maintain their performance. On the other hand, the top-level performers who hold themselves to high standards all have self-drive at an unparalleled level.

Self-drive, often referred to as intrinsic motivation, is the inner force that compels individuals to take initiative, stay determined, and strive for goals without the need for external pressure or constant supervision. It's the capacity to remain focused, disciplined, and proactive in pursuit of personal and professional objectives.

In essence, self-drive is the spark that pushes people to excel, even when faced with challenges. It's about taking ownership of your growth, constantly seeking to improve, and holding yourself accountable for your actions and results. As a leader, especially in law enforcement or other high-stakes fields, self-drive is the foundation of success and sets the tone for those around you.

Self-drive is more than just a desirable quality; it is the foundation for effective leadership. As the motivational speaker Les Brown said, "Shoot for the moon.

Even if you miss, you'll land among the stars." A self-driven leader doesn't wait for external motivation—they create their own momentum, inspiring their teams to reach new heights and ensuring the mission is always moving forward.

Remember, self-drive is not something you are born with; it is a skill you can cultivate and strengthen over time. The more you practice self-discipline, goal-setting, and reflection, the greater your inner drive will become. In law enforcement, this can be the difference between good leadership and transformational leadership.

Excellent and Elite performers are motivated from within. They don't need anyone to push them because they are constantly pushing themselves. Self-drive is the critical element that separates the top 10% and the top 1% from the rest of the pack.

How Standards Relates to the Five Simple Truths

Direction: Standards are tied to direction because the level of performance required must align with the goal. If the direction is not clear, it's impossible to establish meaningful standards. High standards flow from a clear, focused direction.

Intentionality: Setting and upholding high standards requires a deep sense of intentionality. A leader must be deliberate about defining expectations and holding everyone accountable, including themselves. Without intentionality, standards will slip, and mediocrity will creep in.

Teams: Teams thrive when clear standards are in place. When the whole team knows what's expected of them, it's easier to work together cohesively. Standards set the foundation for a high-performing team. They also separate the Good from the Excellent and the Elite from the rest.

Getting Ahead of Your Day: Standards set the expectations for productivity. To get ahead of your day, you must operate with clear standards. If you don't hold yourself accountable to a high standard, your productivity will be inconsistent, and you will always feel like you're catching up.

Raising Standards for Yourself and Your Team

- Identify Standards Early: Assess where your team members fall on the Poor to Elite spectrum and tailor your leadership approach accordingly.
- Encourage Self-Drive: Develop ways to foster self-motivation within your team by setting clear, meaningful goals and celebrating progress.
- Challenge Comfort Zones: Push Good performers out of their comfort zones. Help them understand that staying "good" is not enough.
- Reward Excellence: Recognize and reward those who consistently operate at the

Excellent level. Public acknowledgment of their efforts can motivate others.

- Provide Opportunities for Growth: For Elite performers, create opportunities for leadership, innovation, and challenges that keep them engaged.
- Provide Resources: Provide the necessary resources that exemplify the high standards you aspire to achieve. Don't expect employees to be Excellent without the appropriate training and equipment.

In this chapter, we have explored the five standards—Poor, Average, Good, Excellent, and Elite—and how they relate to motivation, self-drive, and leadership effectiveness. As you reflect on your own leadership journey, consider where you currently stand and where you want to be. Do you hold yourself to an Elite standard, or is there room to grow?

"

Getting Ahead of Your Day doesn't just mean waking up early (though that helps)— it's about intentionality, another key truth. It's setting the agenda for yourself and your team, understanding priorities, and anticipating obstacles. This not only allows you to tackle problems more effectively, but also helps you avoid unnecessary stress. It's about scheduling you into your day.

Chapter 5
Getting Ahead of Your Day: The Fifth Simple Truth

LEADERSHIP IS NOT ABOUT REACTING—IT'S about anticipating. Being proactive, not reactive, is what separates the great leaders from the average ones. The concept of "getting ahead of your day" is about controlling what you can and planning for what you can't. It's about you taking control of your day.

Most people start their day reacting to the demands of others—emails, texts, sudden meetings—and before they know it, they're chasing their tails. Successful leaders, however, begin their day by setting a course of action and sticking to it as much as possible. This can be very difficult for everyone, not just leaders. Due to the demands of life, we seem to be constantly chasing our day and letting the events of the day dictate our position not only organizationally but personally. Many leaders (I have been one of them) let the events around them control them. They run from meeting to meeting, call to call, and one fire to the next. So busy that they see clearly what's happening around them but don't stop to see what's happening to them. They are becoming subservient to their schedule and day. The events of the day make the day. This can lead to disastrous long-term results. Leaders who continually chase their day find themselves doing the urgent not the important. I have found that this last statement is the most under-appreciated truth, yet it is one of the most transformative. When you own your day, rather than letting your day own you, you create confidence, clarity, and calmness for yourself and your team.

Why Getting Ahead of Your Day Matters

Getting Ahead of Your Day doesn't just mean waking up early (though that helps)—it's about intentionality, another key truth. It's setting the agenda for yourself and your team, understanding priorities, and anticipating obstacles. This not only allows you to tackle problems more effectively, but also helps you avoid unnecessary stress. It's about scheduling you into your day.

Getting Ahead of Your Day means preparing for success. Think about an athlete getting ready for a championship game. They don't just show up on game day and hope for the best. They plan, they strategize, they visualize success, and they're prepared for multiple scenarios. Leadership requires the same mindset—each day is your championship day. Let's discuss how we can Get Ahead of Your Day.

The Three Pillars of Getting Ahead of Your Day

1. Preparation
2. Prioritization
3. Proactive Momentum

1. Preparation: The Key to Success

Preparation is the foundation of any successful day. Dwight D. Eisenhower famously said, "In preparing for battle, I have always found that plans are useless, but planning is indispensable." As a general and later president of the United States, Eisenhower knew firsthand that preparation gave him the mental agility to respond to unforeseen events. Even when things don't go according to plan, having a roadmap provides a sense of direction that keeps you from being over-whelmed.

When I talk about Getting Ahead of Your Day, I don't mean simply having a to-do list. I'm talking about mentally setting yourself up for success. This can be as simple as the concept that Admiral McRaven made famous: "make your bed." By making your bed, you complete a simple task that sets the tone, and no matter what happens, you come home to a made bed. This means anticipating challenges and preparing solutions in advance. Just like a military leader before a mission, you must know your objectives and what resources you need to succeed.

How You Can Prepare for Your Day Effectively

Start the night before: Successful leaders don't wait until the morning to think about their day. Spend five to ten minutes each evening reviewing what's coming up. What is the most important task tomorrow? Where might you encounter resistance or difficulty? If you know what's ahead, you can prepare mentally and logistically to handle it.

Morning routine: Before you pick up your phone or dive into emails, take a few minutes for yourself. Meditate, read something inspirational, or journal. This time is about centering yourself and getting into the right mindset. As we referenced earlier, Admiral McRaven said in his famous speech, "If you want to change the world, start off by making your bed." A morning routine sets the tone for a productive day. It's a small, simple victory that creates positive momentum. This simple task has changed my morning routine and has contributed greatly to creating a process that ensures I stay ahead of my day.

2. Prioritization: Focus on What Really Matters

As a leader, your time is your most valuable resource. The most successful leaders know how to prioritize. They focus on the tasks that have the highest impact, both for themselves and their teams. Prioritization is about discerning what's truly important versus what's just urgent.

Stephen Covey, in his book, *7 Habits of Highly Effective People*, differentiates between what's "urgent" and what's "important." Urgent tasks demand your immediate attention (like emails or phone calls), but they may not move you closer to your goals. Important tasks, on the other hand, are the ones that align with your objectives and long-term success. Getting Ahead of Your Day means focusing on what matters most—not just what's calling for your attention. People who chase their day tend to do the urgent and not the important.

How to Prioritize Effectively

Identify your top three tasks: At the start of each day, or the night before, identify the three most important things you need to accomplish. These are the tasks that will move you and your team forward. Tackle them first thing in the morning when you're at your freshest. Save the less important tasks—like checking emails or returning phone calls—for later in the day.

Learn to say no: As a leader, you will be pulled in many directions. Learning to say no, or how to delegate, is crucial to staying focused on your priorities. Remember, just because something is urgent doesn't mean it's your responsibility.

3. Proactive Momentum: Building the Habit of Staying Ahead

Momentum is a powerful force in leadership. Once you start your day off on the right foot, you're more likely to maintain that positive energy throughout the day. However, the opposite is also true. If you start your day in reactive mode—answering emails, dealing with small problems—you set a reactive tone for the rest of the day. You will be playing catch-up, constantly putting out fires instead of focusing on the big picture.

Create proactive momentum: This means planning your actions in advance, taking control of your time, and maintaining a steady pace. You're not just working harder—you're working smarter, ensuring that you're not blindsided by the unexpected.

Schedule proactive blocks of time: Set aside dedicated time blocks for proactive work. For instance, schedule your most important task of the day between 9-11 a.m., when you're most focused. During this time, eliminate distractions—no phone calls, emails, or meetings. This dedicated time allows you to tackle your most pressing tasks before the day starts to spiral out of control.

Anticipate challenges: In leadership, challenges will always arise. The difference between a good leader and a great one is the ability to anticipate problems before they happen. Spend time thinking about potential roadblocks and develop contingency plans for how you will handle them.

Leadership Takeaway

McRaven's philosophy is straightforward yet profound and is a great example of starting small: starting your day by making your bed sets the tone for the rest of the day. This small, intentional act creates a sense of order, accomplishment, and discipline before anything else unfolds. As McRaven said, "If you make your bed every morning, you will have accomplished the first task of the day. It will give you a small sense of pride, and it will encourage you to do another task and another and another."

McRaven's habit of starting the day with purpose underscores the essence of Getting Ahead of Your Day. For leaders, this concept extends beyond making your bed—it's about beginning the day with clarity and intentionality. Whether it's dedicating quiet time to plan your priorities, organizing your workspace, or tackling a critical task early, starting strong sets the tone for the rest of the day.

Admiral McRaven's example demonstrates that even small, deliberate actions can create the foundation for significant accomplishments. As leaders, getting ahead of your day is not just about being prepared for the tasks ahead—it's about taking control, building momentum, and setting a standard for excellence from the very first moment.

Another way to get ahead of your day is to delay reading your emails and text from work before you are ready to tackle the challenge(s) they offer. Many, if not all, of us reach for our phone as our first act of the day. This may occur because your alarm is set on your phone, but it can lead to an automatic response to check other areas. The messages on your phone early in the morning are usually yesterday's and today's problems. This can lead to major frustration and aggravation if we start our day before we are prepared to deal with them. If someone is texting or emailing from the night before or early morning, it generally is a signal that you can wait to respond. If you are in a position that requires you to be available and responsive 24 hours a day, this can be challenging. I know I spent about 95% of my career in a role like this, but I assure you that taking the time to get ahead of your day will make the difference in responding and reacting. Responding is getting ahead of your day; reacting is chasing it.

HOW GETTING AHEAD OF YOUR DAY RELATES TO THE FIVE SIMPLE TRUTHS

Direction: You can't get ahead of your day if you don't know what direction you're heading. Setting daily priorities that align with your larger goals is essential for staying ahead. A clear sense of direction allows you to organize your day for maximum productivity.

Intentionality: Getting ahead of your day requires intentional planning. You need to be deliberate about how you spend your time, ensuring that your actions align with your goals. Without intentionality, you'll find yourself reacting to the day's demands rather than controlling your progress.

Teams: A well-organized team gets ahead of the day together. A leader who helps their team plan ahead and anticipate challenges ensures that the team works efficiently. This builds trust and cohesion within the group.

Standards: High standards are necessary for Getting Ahead of Your Day. When you hold yourself to a higher standard, you set the expectation that you will be proactive, not reactive. This means planning your day to avoid the chaos that comes with disorganization and lack of foresight.

Leadership Tips: How to Get Ahead of Your Day

- Start planning the night before: Review your next day's schedule and prioritize your top three tasks.
- Create a morning routine: Give yourself time to mentally and physically prepare for the day ahead. This will help you start with focus and energy.
- Batch your tasks: Group similar tasks together to work more efficiently (e.g., emails, phone calls).
- Focus on proactive tasks first: Spend the first few hours of your day working on your most important goals.
- Anticipate challenges: Plan for obstacles

before they happen and create contingency strategies to address them.

Final Thoughts: The Impact of Getting Ahead of Your Day

The power of Getting Ahead of Your Day lies in its ability to transform not just your daily habits but your overall leadership effectiveness. When you control your time and focus on what matters most, you set yourself up for long-term success. Leaders who master this truth consistently rise above the rest because they are not playing catch-up—they are proactively creating their future.

Remember, each day presents new opportunities for success or failure. By embracing the simple truth of Getting Ahead of Your Day, you put yourself in the driver's seat, ensuring that you and your team are always moving toward your goals with clarity, purpose, and momentum.

"

Significant leadership requires courage—
courage to set a clear direction even
when the path is uncertain, to act with
intentionality in the face of distractions, to
build and nurture teams that reflect shared
values, to uphold high standards even
when it's difficult, and to prepare each day
with purpose.

Conclusion: Leading with Significance

LEADERSHIP IS MORE THAN A ROLE; IT IS A responsibility—a calling to create positive change in the lives of others. One of my favorite quotes comes from Mike Tomlin, the extremely successful coach of the Pittsburgh Steelers, who in 18 years has never had a losing season, says, "Leaders should never resist the responsibility of leadership."

As we conclude our journey through the Five Simple Truths, remember that being a leader is a constant journey of learning, growing, service, and the pursuit of significance. It is never a destination.

Each truth—Direction, Intentionality, Teams, Standards, and Getting Ahead of Your Day—offers a pillar upon which exceptional leadership is built. These truths are simple, yet their consistent application can transform ordinary leaders into extraordinary ones.

The Legacy of Significance

Success in leadership is admirable, but it is fleeting without a lasting impact. True significance lies in the ability to uplift others, cultivate potential, and create a legacy that inspires future generations. Leaders like Nelson Mandela, General Colin Powell, and Malala Yousafzai exemplify the enduring power of significant leadership. They remind us that leadership is not about titles or accolades but about integrity, courage, and the capacity to inspire others toward a higher purpose.

Significant leadership requires courage—courage to set a clear direction even when the path is uncertain, to act with intentionality in the face of distractions, to build and nurture teams that reflect shared values, to uphold high standards even when it's difficult, and to prepare each day with purpose.

A Challenge to Leaders

As you reflect on the lessons in this book, ask yourself:

- Are my actions aligned with my values and vision?
- Am I intentional in my decisions and leadership approach?
- Do I prioritize relationships and the development of those I lead?
- Have I set and communicated the high standards necessary for excellence?

- Am I proactive, or am I allowing the day to dictate my leadership?

The answers to these questions will guide your next steps. Leadership is not about perfection; it is about progress—deliberate, meaningful progress.

The Five Simple Truths are more than principles; they are tools for transformation. Use them not just to lead but to inspire, not just to achieve but to empower. Commit to these truths and you will not only improve your leadership, but you will also enrich the lives of those you serve.

In the words of John Maxwell:

"Success is when I add value to myself. Significance is when I add value to others."

Let your leadership journey be one of significance. Go forth with purpose, lead with heart, and leave a legacy that stands the test of time.

A Workbook for Success
The Five Simple Truths of Leadership

Introduction: How to Use This Workbook

Leadership isn't just about managing others—it's about managing yourself first. This workbook is designed to help you internalize and apply *The Five Simple Truths of Leadership* through guided exercises, reflection prompts, and practical application steps.

Start with the Main Book

Begin your exploration by reading the main book, *The Five Simple Truths of Leadership*. You will find the core concepts and components in the book. This workbook is meant to be a companion to help you discover how to use the Truths and apply them to your organization, employees, and yourself.

Follow the Workbook Structure

The workbook is designed to follow the contents of the book. Progress through the workbook in the order of the Five Simple Truths.

Participate in the Practical Exercises

Each section of the workbook contains practical exercises that have proven to get the most from the content. These exercises are designed to help you apply the information in the book to your life and organizations. Dedicate the appropriate time to complete the exercises and answer the questions.

Maintain a Workbook Journal

Journaling is the best way to keep track of your thoughts and how you are progressing. This may seem a little much when you are working through the workbook, but it will serve as a great way to right down additional thoughts that will serve you well as you progress through the workbook.

Share and Discuss What You Are Learning

Discuss with co-workers or associates what you are learning in the workbook. The best way to continue learning is to share with others the material and content that is making a positive difference in your life.

Follow Up and Follow Through

Use the material in the book and workbook to create momentum in your learning and growing. Continue to review the material in both and apply the Five Simple Truths to your organizations and life. Use the content and exercises to create a learning environment around you.

Exercises

Each exercise includes **detailed explanations** on how to complete them, followed by **expanded answer spaces** to record your responses. By the end of this workbook, you will have a personalized action plan for leadership success.

The Five Simple Truths of Leadership

1. **Direction** – Leadership begins with clarity of purpose. A leader must know where they are going before they can guide others.
2. **Intentionality** – Leadership is not accidental. It requires deliberate choices and consistent effort.
3. **Teams** – No leader succeeds alone. Building and nurturing a strong team is at the heart of significant leadership.
4. **Standards** – Great leaders hold themselves and their teams to high standards. They push for excellence and create environments where it is the norm.
5. **Getting Ahead of Your Day** – Leadership thrives on preparation. Significant leaders don't wait for the day to dictate their actions; they set the tone from the start.

These Five Simple Truths serve as the foundation of significant leadership, guiding leaders toward a path of clarity, intentionality, collaboration, excellence, and preparation.

Truth 1: Direction – The Compass for Leadership

Direction is one of the most fundamental human needs —it is as essential to our well-being as food or shelter. Deep within us is an innate desire to move forward, to make progress, and to find purpose in the journey. Every waking moment of our lives, whether we realize it or not, we're always heading somewhere. The moment you wake up, your day begins to unfold along a certain path. By the time your head hits the pillow at night, your mind is already churning about what's next.

Direction provides more than just a path—it offers clarity. It eliminates the noise of distractions and competing priorities, allowing you to focus on what truly matters. This clarity builds momentum, and with momentum comes progress. Leaders with direction inspire confidence because they know where they are going and can articulate why it matters.

Exercise: Where Are You Going?

1. Describe your current position in life and leadership.

2. What would you say is your current direction as a person and as a leader?

3. Define your vision for yourself.

4. What are your short term goals for the next year? Name at least three.

5. List three obstacles preventing you from reaching these goals.

Expanded Answer Space:

Activity: Crafting Your Leadership Statement

Using your responses from the previous exercise, create a **Leadership Mission Statement** that clearly defines your approach to leadership. Keep it simple and clear.

Truth 2: Intentionality – Taking Purposeful Action

In the fast-paced world we live in, it's easy to get caught up in the whirlwind of activity without ever stopping to ask, "Is this getting me closer to where I want to be?" "Am I getting closer to what I need to be doing to make me the best leader possible?" Questions like these are examples of why the second Simple Truth —Intentionality—is so crucial. Intentionality is about acting with purpose and making deliberate choices that align with your direction. The law of intentionality is simple: "What you tend to set your mind to gets done." This is a truth that cannot be understated. Simple acts of intentionality on a consistent basis can improve your results dramatically.

One of the most dangerous traps leaders fall into is busyness. You might think that by staying busy, you're being productive, but in reality, busy work is often the enemy of progress. As the legendary Stoic philosopher Seneca said, "We suffer more often in imagination than in reality." In leadership, the same holds true: we often fill our time with tasks that seem urgent but have little bearing on our actual success. Intentionality demands that you stop, think, and make decisions based on where you want to go. Intentionality is putting action into thoughts. We have thousands and thousands of thoughts a day. If we don't become intentional regarding those thoughts, they stay trapped. Intentionality frees our thoughts from the confines of our minds.

Exercise: The Impact of Daily Choices

1. Write down three intentional decisions you made today.

2. Did these decisions align with your goals? Why or why not?

3. What is one way you can be more intentional tomorrow?

4. Describe a time in your life that you were more intentional with your actions and what was the result?

Expanded Answer Space: Make a list of things you will be more intentional about.

Truth 3: Teams – Leadership Through Collaboration

Teams amplify a leader's vision and success. Understanding the roles within a team is essential for strong leadership. Leadership is never a solo endeavor. While stories of individual brilliance often capture our imagination, the truth is that no significant achievement happens in isolation. Behind every great leader is a team—a collective force driving the mission forward. Teams amplify the leader's vision, provide diverse perspectives, and turn plans into action. Without them, even the most determined leader will fall short of their potential.

Building and sustaining effective teams, however, remains one of the most challenging aspects of leadership. Reflecting on my own journey, many of my leadership struggles were rooted in two critical issues: either I did not have the right team in place, or I failed to fully develop and unlock the potential of the team. Building effective teams can prove to be very challenging, but it will be worth every minute you spend.

Exercise: The Three Types of Teams in Your Life

1. List examples of what makes you a good Team of One. (Example: self confident, personal values, resilient, good life balance, hold myself to high standards, know my strengths and weaknesses.)

2. List of examples where you are a good Team of Two. (Examples: workout partner, mentor or mentee, work well with other team members, willing to sacrifice for others.)

3. List examples of how you are a Team of We? (Examples: understand the mission of my organization, willing to make tough decisions for the greater good, works for the greater good of my organization.)

Expanded Answer Space: Write about a time you were a valued member of a team.

Truth 4: Standards – The Foundation of Excellence

Having high standards is the key to high performance. I have done many things in my life like most of you, but when I hold myself to the highest standards, I accomplish the most. When you hold yourself to high standards, you will always like the results. In leadership, it is easy to talk about having standards. But, as with most things in life, the real challenge lies in holding yourself and others to those standards consistently. The Fourth Simple Truth is all about setting the bar for excellence—and beyond.

As a leader, I have often been told—and I have long believed—that setting clear expectations is the foundation of creating performance, motivation, and results. And there's a certain truth in that. Expectations give people a framework to understand their roles and responsibilities, providing direction for their efforts. But I have found there is more than setting expectations to get the most out of ourselves and others.

Exercise: Setting Your Leadership Standards

1. Name the five leadership standards from the book

and write a short example of how you have seen them in your own leadership efforts.

2. Do your current habits align with the highest standards? Why or why not?

3. How do you plan on holding yourself to the highest standards?

4. If you are in a leadership role, how do you plan on holding others to the highest standards?

Expanded Answer Space: Write a few daily things you can do to hold yourself to the highest standards.

Truth 5: Getting Ahead of Your Day – Proactive Leadership

Leadership is not about reacting—it's about anticipating. Being proactive, not reactive, is what separates the great leaders from the average ones. The concept of "getting ahead of your day" is about controlling what you can and planning for what you can't. It's about you taking control of your day.

Most people start their day reacting to the demands of others—emails, texts, sudden meetings—and before they know it, they're chasing their tails. Successful leaders, however, begin their day by setting a course of action and sticking to it as much as possible. This can be very difficult for everyone, not just leaders. Due to the demands of life, we seem to be constantly chasing our day and letting the events of the day dictate our position not only organizationally but personally. Many leaders (I have been one of them) let the events around them control them. They run from meeting to meeting, call to call, and one fire to the next. So busy that they see clearly what's happening around them but don't stop to see what's happening to them. They are becoming subservient to their schedule and day. The events of the day make the day. This can lead to disastrous long-term results. Leaders who continually chase their day find themselves doing the urgent not the important. I have found that this last statement is the most under-appreciated truth, yet it is one of the most transformative. When you own your day, rather than letting your day own you, you create confidence, clarity, and calmness for yourself and your team.

Exercise: Identifying Your Distractions

1. Write down everything that distracted you in the past 24 hours.

2. How can you eliminate or reduce these distractions?

3. Name at least three things that you can do in the morning that will help you get ahead of your day.

4. Getting ahead of your day also means preparing yourself for meetings and important tasks. Name at least three things you can do to better prepare yourself before meetings and before starting those important tasks.

Expanded Answer Space: List any other things you can do to get ahead of your day.

Final Reflection & Action Plan

1. What are the top three lessons you've learned from this workbook?

2. How will you apply the Five Simple Truths to Your Leadership and Life?

3. Write your Leadership Commitment Statement:
Example: "I commit to leading with purpose, setting high standards, and being intentional in my actions every day."

Expanded Answer Space:

This workbook is designed to help you **internalize, apply, and grow** in your leadership journey. Use it consistently, reflect deeply, and take action. **Your journey to significance starts now!**

Bibliography

Books and Resources

Covey, Stephen R. *The 7 Habits of Highly Effective People: Powerful Lessons in Personal Change*. New York: Free Press, 1989.

Gollwitzer, Peter M. "Implementation Intentions: Strong Effects of Simple Plans." *American Psychologist* 54, no. 7 (1999): 493–503. https://doi.org/10.1037/0003-066X.54.7.493.

Maxwell, John C. *The 21 Irrefutable Laws of Leadership: Follow Them and People Will Follow You*. Nashville: Harper Collins Leadership, 2007.

Maxwell, John C. *The 5 Levels of Leadership: Proven Steps to Maximize Your Potential*. Nashville: Harper Collins Leadership, 2011.

Seneca. *Letters from a Stoic*. Translated by Robin Campbell. London: Penguin Classics, 1997. (Original work written ca. 65 CE).

Tzu, Lao. *Tao Te Ching*. Translated by Stephen Mitchell. New York: Harper Perennial Modern Classics, 2005. (Original work written ca. 500 BCE).

Speeches and Statements

McRaven, William H. "Make Your Bed: Admiral McRaven's Commencement Speech at the University of Texas." University of Texas. Accessed February 28, 2025. https://www.utexas.edu.

Washington, George. "Valley Forge Strategies." 1777-1778. [Historical context summarized].

Notable Figures and Contextual Case Studies

Powell, Colin. *My American Journey*. New York: Random House, 1995.

Mandela, Nelson. *Long Walk to Freedom: The Autobiography of Nelson Mandela*. New York: Little, Brown and Company, 1995.

Bibliography

Musk, Elon. Leadership at SpaceX, referenced from public interviews and business strategies (various online sources).

Other Quotes and Attributions

Washington, Denzel. "Don't Confuse Movement with Progress." Public speech, various recordings.

Lombardi, Vince. *What It Takes to Be Number One: Vince Lombardi on Leadership*. New York: McGraw-Hill, 1997.

Aurelius, Marcus. *Meditations*. Translated by Gregory Hays. New York: Modern Library, 2002. (Original work written ca. 180 CE).

Wright, Frank Lloyd. Inspirational quote about belief in action. Various publications on Wright's work and philosophy.

Index

Index

Index

Index

About the Author

Dean Crisp is a highly awarded 38-year veteran of law enforcement including 21 years in command leadership positions and 17 years as a chief of police.

After his retirement in 2009, Dean became an Instructor as well as the National Training Director for FBI-LEEDA (FBI Law Enforcement Executive Development Association).

In 2018, he founded Leaders Helping Leaders Network (LHLN); as the founder and CEO of LHLN, Dean currently stays busy training the next generation of leaders with his *Intentional Leadership*, *Servant Officer*, and *Master Leadership* curriculum throughout the U.S. and Canada. Learn more about Dean, his upcoming classes and speaking engagements at: www.lhln.org.

Also by Dean Crisp

Essential Leadership Lessons from the Thin Blue Line

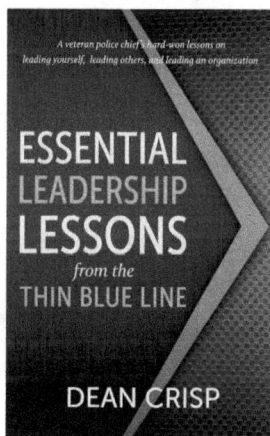

A veteran police chief's hard-won lessons on leading yourself, leading others, and leading an organization.

Essential Leadership Lessons from the Thin Blue Line is just that – lessons learned the old-fashioned way through trial and error, studying, hard work, and experience while on our nation's front lines to serve and protect. Dean Crisp spent decades leading people where a single misstep could cost a life. Faced with the daily challenges of a police chief, Dean threw himself into learning all he could about effective leadership and applying those lessons in his departments. He shares those hard-won lessons in this book.

Essential Leadership Lessons from the Thin Blue Line uses personal anecdotes to drive home the human element of leadership and will connect with you at any point on your journey to becoming a significant leader.

The Leadership Recipe

What if there was a recipe you could follow that would help develop you into the leader you've always wanted to be? No matter your ambition—whether you want to lead your department well or an entire organization as CEO —the components of leadership presented in this book are designed to help you grow into the best leader you can be. This allegory offers a refreshing way to help leaders at all levels understand the ingredients of successful leadership for themselves and others.

from the bestselling author of
Essential Leadership Lessons from the Thin Blue Line

THE

LEADERSHIP

RECIPE

DEAN CRISP

www.ingramcontent.com/pod-product-compliance
Lightning Source LLC
Chambersburg PA
CBHW070657190326
41458CB00053B/6912/J

* 9 7 8 1 6 1 1 5 3 6 9 1 1 *